W9-AVK-717

A DEVOTIONAL *For Little Ones*

Praise and Worship

A DEVOTIONAL *For Little Ones*

Praise and Worship

WORD PUBLISHING
Dallas · London · Vancouver · Melbourne

This book was written by Angela and Ken Abraham. The Abrahams co-authored the award-winning *Hosanna Bible*. Angela is a freelance writer and was formerly a children's church coordinator for Christ Church in Nashville, Tennessee. Ken is author of more than twenty books. The Abrahams have two daughters, Ashleigh and Alyssa.

Illustrations are by Terry Anderson and Kathleen Dunne through Rosenthal Represents, Los Angeles, California.

PRAISE AND WORSHIP
A Devotional for Little Ones

Scripture quotations are from the *International Children's Bible, New Century Version*, copyright © 1983, 1986, 1988, Word Publishing.

Managing Editor: Laura Minchew   Project Editor: Beverly Phillips

Library of Congress Cataloging-in-Publication Data

Abraham, Angela, 1958–
    Praise and worship, a devotional for little ones / Angela and Ken Abraham ;
illustrated by Terry Anderson and Kathleen Dunne.
        p.   cm.
    ISBN 0-8499-1191-5
    1. Children—Prayer-books and devotions—English.   2. Christian life—Juvenile
literature.   I. Abraham, Ken.   II. Anderson, Terry, ill.   III. Dunne, Kathleen, 1933–
IV. Title.
BV4870.A26   1996
242'.62—dc20

                                                                              96–13343
                                                                                    CIP
                                                                                     AC

Printed in Hong Kong

98 99 00 PPI 9 8 7 6 5 4 3

THE LORD'S PRAYER

"Our Father in heaven,

we pray that your name will always be
   kept holy.

We pray that your kingdom will come.

We pray that what you want will be done,
   here on earth as it is in heaven.

Give us the food we need for each day.

Forgive the sins we have done,
   just as we have forgiven those who did
   wrong to us.

Do not cause us to be tested; but save us
   from the Evil One."

—MATTHEW 6:9–13

God wants me to pray, praise, and thank Him
no matter how I feel . . . what I do . . .
where I go . . . or who I'm with.

CONTENTS

HOW I FEEL

"Praise the Lord. He heard my prayer for help. The Lord is my strength and shield. I trust him, and he helps me. I am very happy. And I praise him with my song." —PSALM 28:6–7

WHAT I DO

"Lord, teach me your ways. Guide me to do what is right. . . ." —PSALM 27:11

WHERE I GO

"Lord . . . You know all about me. You know where I go and where I lie down. You know well everything I do. Your knowledge is amazing to me. It is more than I can understand." —PSALM 139:1, 3, 6

WHO I AM WITH

"The Lord is great. He is worthy of our praise. . . . The Lord will keep his promises. With love he takes care of all he has made. . . . The Lord is close to everyone who prays to him." —PSALM 145:3, 13, 18

INDEX

HOW TO USE THIS BOOK

Dear Parents,

In writing *Praise and Worship, a Devotional for Little Ones,* we have tried to create an exciting way for children ages three to eight to celebrate God's love and care for them every day. We have chosen a variety of songs, Bible stories, poems, activities, and prayers to show children *how to praise God no matter how they feel, where they go, what they do, or who they are with.*

Each chapter is divided into five sections: **Praise, Prayer, Promise, People in the Bible,** and **Pleasing God.**

First is the **Praise** section. Starting your time together with praise will help your child learn to keep his or her gaze on God instead of on the gifts he or she hopes to get from Him. You and your child can explore various ways of praising God.

Sometimes you will praise Him through a song, sometimes with a poem, or a prayer. At times your praise will be noisy as you clap your hands, march, play homemade instruments, and shout. At other times, you will simply be still and know that He is our almighty God. Can you imagine what it does to the heart of our heavenly Father to hear the voices of our children giving Him praise?

Next, you will find suggestions for talking to God in **Prayer**. These prayers include prayer poems, prayers from the Bible, and modern-day prayers. This section will help children know they can pray anytime, anywhere, in groups, or alone. Their prayers can be aloud or silent, long or short.

Children will learn to talk to God about anything . . . and everything! They will learn to talk to God when they are happy, sad, lonely, afraid, or angry, and they will tell God how they feel. They will thank Him for friends, family, flowers, and fun times. They will learn that whatever they do or wherever they go, they can talk to God. They can pray on the way to school or on a ball field, just as easily as they can pray at church. Children will learn that prayer is more than reciting words to God. It is sharing with Him from the heart. It is listening for His voice and obeying what He says.

The third section in each chapter is a Bible **Promise**. One way God speaks to us is through His Word. You may want your child to memorize these encouraging verses from Scripture. Take some time each day to think about these truths. This will help your child understand what it means to "wait upon the Lord" and to watch and listen for answers to their prayers.

Fourth is a section describing **People in the Bible**. This is a Bible story illustrating the main point in each chapter. It is also the passage of Scripture on which the truth being emphasized is based. Children will learn to obey God's Word by following the examples of the people in the Bible.

Each chapter ends with a **Pleasing God** section which includes fun activities such as making a *thankful necklace* or a *prayer album*, or doing a simple finger play or action rhyme. These practical applications will help bring the Bible truths to life in an easy-to-remember way.

It is our hope that this book will lay a foundation in tender, young hearts for a growing, thriving relationship with God. As you learn to praise God with your child, you too will become encouraged! As you learn to pray together, your faith in God will become stronger. Remember God has promised to bless you as you praise Him. And God always keeps His promises!

ANGELA AND KEN ABRAHAM

I PRAISE GOD FOR HIS LOVE

What is the best gift you've ever been given? Have you ever thought of Jesus as a gift? God has! God showed His love for you by sending Jesus to be your Savior.

How can you show God you are thankful for His gift of love?

Praise

Sing this chorus to the tune of "Ring Around the Rosy."

God's Love Is Amazing

God's love is amazing.
Children thank and praise Him,
Love Him, serve Him—
Let's all bow down.

Ask a parent, brother, sister, or friend to sing this chorus with you. "Praisers" form a circle holding hands. As you sing the chorus, circle to the left (clockwise). At the end of the song, drop your hands and kneel down. Bow your head and fold your hands as though you are praying.

1

Prayer

Father, We Thank Thee

Father, we thank Thee for the night,
And for the pleasant morning light,
For rest and food and loving care,
And all that makes the world so fair.

Help us to do the things we should,
To be to others kind and good,
In all we do and all we say,
To grow more loving every day.
                    —AUTHOR UNKNOWN

Promise

". . . we should love each other, because love comes from God. The person who loves has become God's child and knows God. Whoever does not love does not know God, because God is love."
                    —1 JOHN 4:7–8

People in the Bible

Mary and Martha held a dinner to honor Jesus. Martha served the food. Lazarus ate with Jesus.

Mary did something special to show Jesus how much she loved Him. Mary knew that Jesus was God's holy Son.

Mary poured a jar of costly perfume on Jesus' head and feet. Then she wiped His feet with her hair. The smell of sweet perfume filled the room.

Jesus' followers said Mary was foolish to waste the
expensive perfume. They complained, "The perfume should
be sold and the money given to the poor."

Jesus' followers did not understand Mary's actions. But Jesus
was pleased with Mary's gift of love. "Leave her alone,"
said Jesus. "Mary did the right thing."

Mary had given praise to God by her act of kindness.

Pleasing God

Mary showed her love for Jesus by giving Him the best gift she had. Mary was thankful for Jesus, her Savior. She praised God for His gift of love.

How can you show Jesus you love Him?

How can you share God's love with others?

Try making a *heart filled with love.* Draw a big, red heart on white construction paper. Draw a picture of Jesus inside the heart. Cut out the heart. Give your heart to someone you love. Remember to tell him or her about God's gift of love!

I PRAISE GOD WHEN I AM HAPPY

Let's think some happy thoughts together.

I feel happy when I _____.

I can make others happy when I _____.

How can you make God happy?

Praise

Sing this chorus to the tune of "The More We Get Together."

Praise God When I Am Happy

Praise God when I am happy, I'm happy, I'm happy.
Praise God when I am happy. I thank God today.
I share with my brother. We help one another.
Praise God when I am happy. I thank God this way.

Praise God when I'm not happy, not happy, not happy.
Praise God when I'm not happy. I thank God anyway.
I listen to my father. I obey my mother.
Praise God when I'm not happy. I thank Him always!

Prayer

Dear Jesus,
Thank You for everything that makes me smile, like chocolate-chip cookies, ice cream, and jelly beans. Thank You for happy thoughts of birthday parties, bunny rabbits, and baseball. I thank You for happy times on bikes, vacations, and picnics. Most of all, I thank You for friends to laugh with and family to love!

> *Love,*
> *Me*

Promise

"Happy are the people who know how to praise you.
Lord, let them live in the light of your presence.
In your name they rejoice all the time. They praise your goodness."

> —PSALM 89:15–16

People in the Bible

David loved the Lord with all his heart. He happily wrote many songs of praise while caring for his sheep. He sang, "Lord, Your name is the most wonderful name in all the earth. Even children and babies sing praises to You."

David wrote, "Children, come and listen to me. I will teach you to worship the Lord." He sang, "Every good thing I have comes from the Lord."

David said, "I praise the Lord at all times. His praise is always on my lips."

Pleasing God

Would you like to do something that will make someone smile?

Ask your mother if you can help her bake a batch of cutout cookies. Yum! Yum! Remember to thank God before eating, and don't forget to share!

Recipe:

1 cup butter	1/2 teaspoon salt
1 3/4 cup sugar	1 teaspoon baking soda
2 eggs	1 teaspoon baking powder
1 cup sour cream	4 1/2 cups flour
1/2 teaspoon vanilla	

Cream the butter and sugar together; add the eggs, sour cream, and vanilla. Beat until creamy. Combine the salt, soda, baking powder, and flour. Slowly add dry mixture to creamy mixture, stirring after each addition. Chill the dough. Roll out dough and cut into desired shapes with a cookie cutter. Bake at 350 degrees for approximately ten minutes.

A PRAYER WHEN I FEEL SAD

What makes you feel sad? Did you know Jesus gets disappointed, too? What do you think might make Jesus sad?

Praise

Say the words from Psalm 34:1–2 aloud, with the following actions.

"*I* (point to yourself) *will praise the Lord* (raise hands heavenward) *at all times. His praise is always on my lips* (point to lips). *My whole being* (cross hands over your heart) *praises the Lord* (raise hands heavenward)."

11

Prayer

Dear Lord,
Open up a window,
  in the cellar of my soul.
Let me walk in sunshine,
  wherever I may go.
Lift my thoughts toward heaven
  and gently let me know.
That You are walking with me
  wherever I may go.
In Jesus' Name, amen.

Promise

"Always be happy. Never stop praying.
Give thanks whatever happens.
That is what God wants for you in Christ Jesus."
                    —1 THESSALONIANS 5:16–18

People in the Bible

On the way to Jerusalem, Jesus met ten men. Their bodies were covered with ugly sores, and they were very sad. They had left their families and friends so others would not catch their disease.

"Master, please help us!" they called.

Jesus said, "Go and show the priests that you are healed."

As the men obeyed Jesus, their sores went away.

13

All the men were happy they were healed. One man hurried back to thank Jesus.

He said, "Glory to God! I'm healed!"

"Ten men were healed," said Jesus. "Where are the other nine?"

Jesus was disappointed that they forgot to praise God for their healing. But He was pleased with the thankful man.

Pleasing God

If you are disappointed about something, try making a *thankful necklace* out of a paper chain.

List several things you are thankful for—your family, food, home, and other things. Draw a picture of each thing you are thankful for on a strip of paper. Glue the ends together, making a circle. Thread the next strip of paper through the circle and glue the ends together, making another circle. Continue adding paper circles until your necklace is large enough to fit over your head.

Wear your *thankful necklace* whenever you feel disappointed. It will help you remember all the things you have to be thankful for!

A PROMISE WHEN I FEEL LONELY

Do you ever feel lonely? Do you know it is possible to be alone, yet not lonely? Jesus is with you all the time, even when no one else is around!

Praise

I would like to play with someone today,
But I am alone with no friends of my own.
Lord, let me reach for Your hand, again,
When I feel lonely and need a friend.
And thank You for listening to my prayer,
It always helps me to know that You care!

Angela Abraham / copyright © 1995 by House of Abraham

Prayer

Dear Jesus,
You are the only One who knows I'm crying. I'm afraid of being by myself. I feel all alone. I'm afraid of strangers. Lord, will You protect me? Please send me a friend. And help me to remember that You are my best Friend. Thank You for never leaving me! Amen.

Promise

". . . God has said, 'I will never leave you; I will never forget you.' So we can feel sure and say, 'I will not be afraid because the Lord is my helper.'"

—HEBREWS 13:5–6

People in the Bible

Elijah came to Mount Sinai, the mountain of God. The Lord said, "Stand in front of Me. I will pass by you." A great wind swept by Elijah, but the Lord was not in it. Elijah saw an earthquake, but the Lord was not in it. A fire passed by, too, but the Lord was not in it either.

After the fire, Elijah heard a soft voice. He knew it was the voice of the Lord. "Why are you running, Elijah?" the Lord asked him.

"I feel afraid and alone," Elijah said. The Lord said, "Go pour holy oil on Elisha. He will be your helper and friend."

Pleasing God

Can you think of someone who may be lonely right now?

____A friend who has   ____A grandma
moved away

____A neighbor   ____A grandpa

The best way to have a friend is to be a friend. How can
you be a friend to someone who is lonely?

____Call him or her   ____Send him or her a
on the phone.   card.

____Write the person   ____Pray for that person.
a letter.

The next time you are feeling lonely, talk to your best
Friend, Jesus. Ask Him how you can help someone else who
may be feeling lonely.

HOW TO PRAY WHEN I AM ANGRY

Have you been angry today? How do you think God feels when you get angry?

Praise

Sing the following song to the tune of "If You're Happy."

> *If you're angry and you know it, stomp your feet*
> (frown; stomp your feet).
> *If you're angry and you know it, stomp your feet*
> (frown; stomp your feet).
> *If you're angry and you know it, then your life will really*
> *show it.*
> *If you're angry and you know it, stomp your feet*
> (frown; stomp your feet).
>
> *If you're happy and you know it, clap your hands*
> (smile; clap your hands).
> *If you're happy and you know it, clap your hands*
> (smile; clap your hands).
> *If you're happy and you know it, then your life will really*
> *show it.*
> *If you're happy and you know it, clap your hands*
> (smile; clap your hands).

Prayer

Dear Lord,

*I know it makes You sad when I get real mad
and start to say things that are bad.*

*Please forgive me today;
Please help me to say
things in a much nicer way.*

In Jesus' Name, amen.

Promise

*"Do not be bitter or angry or mad. . . . You are God's children whom
he loves. So try to be like God. Live a life of love."*

—E<small>PHESIANS</small> *4:31; 5:1–2*

People in the Bible

One day Cain and Abel were worshiping God. They each brought God a gift. Abel's gift was good. But Cain's gift was selfish.

Cain was angry that God did not accept his offering. Cain wanted to kill Abel.

"Your heart is angry," God said. "Do good, and I will accept you."

Cain did not obey God. Cain hit Abel and killed him.

"Where is your brother?" God asked.

Cain yelled, "I don't know. Is it my job to take care of him?"

God said, "I see what you did to your brother. You will be punished for the terrible way you treated him."

God told Cain, "Your heart is evil, so you cannot stay in My presence." Cain roamed the earth without God.

Pleasing God

How did God punish Cain?

How do you think that made Cain feel?

When you get angry, ask Jesus to forgive you. He will make your heart clean.

Why is the boy in this picture so happy now? Next time you take a bath, notice how good it feels to be clean.

Next time you get angry, try blowing soap bubbles. This will remind you to keep your heart clean!

HELP ME WHEN I AM AFRAID

Can you name a time when you were afraid?

1. Going to the doctor
3. Being alone

2. First day of school
4. Other . . .

Did you pray? What happened?

Praise

Whisper a Prayer

Traditional

Arr. Allan Koppelberger

Whis-per a prayer in the morn-ing, Whis-per a prayer at noon; _____ Whis-per a prayer in the eve - ning To keep _____ your heart in tune. _____

Arrangement copyright © 1995 by House of Abraham

26

Prayer

Dear Lord,

I hear thunder crash, and I see lightning flash,
'til I'm scared to open my eyes.

Father, would You please help me by
pushing away these frightening clouds
on this dark, dreary day?

Take away my fear and doubt,
lift up my heart, I pray.

In Jesus' Name, amen.

Promise

"So don't worry, because I am with you. Don't be afraid, because I am
your God. I will make you strong and will help you. I will support you
with my right hand that saves you."

—ISAIAH 41:10

People in the Bible

Esther was the queen in Persia. No one in the palace knew Esther was Jewish. "Keep it secret," said Esther's Cousin Mordecai. Esther always listened to his wise advice.

Haman, the king's officer, hated Mordecai, the Jew. He made an evil plan to get rid of him. He tricked the king into signing a law that called for all Jewish people living in the land to be killed.

Mordecai asked Esther to talk to the king.

Esther was frightened. She said, "There is a law that forbids me from going to the king without being invited. I could be punished."

Mordecai said, "God may have let you be chosen queen for just such a time as this. Please help your people."

Esther prayed that she would not be afraid. The Lord helped Esther. She boldly went to see the king. The king loved Esther and listened to her. The king punished Haman for his hatred of Mordecai. And God used Esther to save her people!

Pleasing God

Are you afraid of something or someone?

Would you like to have courage like Esther?

God will help you when you trust Him.

List several of your fears on a piece of paper. You may want to draw pictures to show the things you are afraid of.

Now tear the paper into as many pieces as you can. Then throw all the pieces into the garbage. Thank Jesus for taking away all of your fears.

A PROMISE WHEN I AM SICK

Where can you go for help when you are sick?

We thank God for hospitals, doctors, and medicine.

But remember, Jesus is the One who really makes us feel better. Always ask Him for His help.

Praise

Read this prayer from Jeremiah 17:14 aloud.

> *"Lord, heal me, and I will truly be healed.*
> *Save me, and I will truly be saved.*
> *Lord, you are the one I praise."*

31

Prayer

Dear Jesus,
When I feel bad, sick, or tired, I will trust You.
Soothe all my aches, and take away the pain. Help me to rest and feel
better. Please help my family and friends not to worry. Bless everyone
who is praying for me. Thank You, Jesus, for healing me! Amen.

Promise

"The Lord will give him strength when he is sick.
The Lord will make him well again."

—Psalm 41:3

People in the Bible

Peter preached in Joppa. A woman named Tabitha lived there. She always helped the poor. And the people loved her dearly. Suddenly Tabitha became sick and died! The believers quickly sent for Peter.

When Peter arrived all the poor widows were crying. The women were sad because their friend had died. They pointed to the beautiful clothes Tabitha had given them. "Look at what Tabitha made for us," the women said.

33

Peter kneeled beside Tabitha. He prayed for her, "Tabitha, rise and be healed!"

She opened her eyes! Then Peter held Tabitha's hand and helped her up. Peter called the widows into the room. They were surprised to find Tabitha sitting up. The widows were happy their dear friend was alive.

Many people in Joppa believed in the Lord when they learned about this miracle.

Pleasing God

When Peter prayed for Tabitha, she was made well. Can you think of someone who might not be feeling well? Why not pray for that person right now?

The next time you are sick, make a list of five things you enjoy doing when you feel well. Draw pictures of yourself doing your favorite things. Remember to thank God for making you well.

Draw a picture or card for someone who is sick.

HOW TO PRAY WHEN I AM WORRIED

What do you worry about? God wants to take care of you.
He promises to give you everything you need.

Praise

Cast Your Cares

Angela Abraham

Angela Abraham
Arr. Allan Koppelberger

Cast your cares up - on the Fa - ther, Cast your cares up - on the
Fa - ther. Throw your wor - ries on the liv - ing wa - ter;
Praise God for what He will do! Cast your cares up - on the Fa - ther,
Cast your cares up - on the Fa - ther. Throw your wor - ries on the
liv - ing wa - ter; be - cause He will car - ry you.

Prayer

Dear Jesus,
I'm worried about doing something I've never done before. I get
scared about going to new places. I'm afraid of being different than
the other children. If someone asks me a question, help me to know
the answer. If I don't understand something, please make me brave
enough to ask for help. Lord, You give me wisdom and courage.
Thank You for giving me everything I need. Amen.

Promises

"My God will use his wonderful riches in Christ Jesus to give you
everything you need."

—PHILIPPIANS 4:19

37

People in the Bible

One day Jesus sat on a hillside and taught His followers. "See the birds in the sky?" He said. "Your heavenly Father feeds them. God helps the lovely flowers to grow, too. If God cares about the birds and flowers, you can trust Him to take care of you, too!"

Pleasing God

Most of the things we worry about never happen. It pleases God when we stop worrying and start trusting Him. Talk to your heavenly Father. He will take care of you.

The birds don't worry. And the flowers don't fret. So why should you? Scatter some birdseed or bread crumbs outside. Watch how the birds eat the food you have given them. Now water some plants or flowers in your garden or house. Talk about some ways God takes care of you.

A PROMISE OF COMFORT

Do you know anyone who feels bad or discouraged today? Jesus promises to comfort us when we feel bad. He will help us in times of trouble.

Praise

Praise Him! Praise Him!

Traditional

Arr. Allan Koppelberger

Praise Him, praise Him, all ye lit-tle chil-dren; God is love, God is love. Praise Him, praise Him, all ye lit-tle chil-dren; God is love, God is love.

Arrangement copyright © 1995 by House of Abraham

40

Prayer

This prayer is based on the Twenty-third Psalm.

Lord,
You are my shepherd; I have everything I need.
You give me rest in green pastures. You lead me to calm
water.
You give me new strength. For the good of Your Name,
You lead me on paths that are right. Even if I walk through
a very dark valley, I will not be afraid because You are
with me.
Your rod and Your walking stick comfort me. You prepare a
meal for me in front of my enemies.
You pour oil on my head.
You give me more than I can hold. Surely Your goodness
and love will be with me all my life.
And I will live in the house of the Lord forever. Amen.

Promise

"God is our protection and our strength.
He always helps in times of trouble!"

—PSALM 46:1

41

People in the Bible

Jesus told His followers, "Children are very important to God." Then Jesus told a story to show how much God loves His children.

"A man had one hundred sheep. One sheep got lost. The man left the other ninety-nine sheep to search for the lost one. He searched everywhere until he found the lost sheep. The man was very happy."

Jesus said, "The shepherd put the sheep on his shoulders and carried it home. In the same way, your heavenly Father does not want any of His children to be lost."

Later, Jesus told His followers, "I am the Good Shepherd. I know My sheep, and My sheep know Me. The Good Shepherd gives His life for the sheep."

43

Pleasing God

Help someone feel better by making him or her a *comfort card*. You may want to draw a picture of a lamb and decorate it with cotton balls.

Think of Jesus, the Good Shepherd, as you prepare your card. When you give your friend this card, tell him or her about the Good Shepherd.

I PRAISE GOD FOR HEARING MY PRAYERS

God always answers your prayers! Sometimes the answer is yes. Sometimes the answer is no. Sometimes the answer is wait awhile. He doesn't always give you what you want. But He gives you what you need.

Praise

Lord, Teach a Little Child to Pray

Lord, teach a little child to pray,
And then accept my prayer.
Thou hearest all the words I say
For Thou art everywhere.

A little sparrow cannot fall
Unnoticed, Lord, by Thee,
And though I am so young and small
Thou dost take care of me.

Teach me to do the thing that's right,
And when I sin, forgive,
And make it still my chief delight
To serve Thee while I live.

—JANE TAYLOR

Prayer

Please give me what I ask, dear Lord,
If You'd be glad about it.
But if You think it's not for me,
Please help me do without it.
                —TRADITIONAL

Promise

"I asked the Lord for help, and he answered me. . . . The Lord sees the good people. He listens to their prayers. . . .
The Lord hears good people when they cry out to him. He saves them from all their troubles."

                —PSALM 34:4, 15, 17

People in the Bible

Hannah wanted a baby very much. She prayed to God for a son.

She promised he would do God's work all his life. Eli, the priest, saw Hannah praying. "Go in peace," he said. "May God answer your prayer." The Lord God blessed Hannah with a baby boy. She named him Samuel, which means "Asked of God."

Hannah rememberd her promise to God. When Samuel was still a small child, she took him to Eli at the Holy Tent. And Samuel lived with the priest. God was pleased with Hannah because she kept her promise. God blessed Hannah with more children. Hannah became the mother of three more sons and two daughters!

Pleasing God

God hears even the simplest prayer. And He will answer by giving what is best for us. Pretend you are calling God on the telephone. What are some of the things you would like to tell Him? Be sure to tell God you love Him. Thank God for all the good things He has given you. God loves to hear from His children.

HELP ME TO BE KIND AND GOOD

Everyone knows it is better to be good rather than bad. But what does it mean to be good? Being good means to live according to God's Word, the Bible. It means being kind and helping others. It means obeying your parents. Name some other ways you can be good.

Praise

Sing these words to the tune of "Mary Had a Little Lamb."

Help Me to Be Kind and Good

Help me to be kind and good,
To always do the things I should;
Give me wisdom from above,
To share with others God's great love.

Prayer

All for You, dear God,
Everything I do,
Or think,
Or say,
The whole day long.
Help me to be good.

—Author Unknown

Promise

"And God gives us the things we ask for. We receive these things
because we obey God's commands, and we do what pleases him."

—1 John 3:22

People in the Bible

Naomi lived in the country of Moab. It was far from her hometown of Bethlehem. Naomi was sad because her husband and sons had died. She decided to move back to Bethlehem. Naomi told her daughter-in-law Ruth, "I am old and poor. You are young and beautiful. Stay here in your own country and remarry."

Naomi was a good woman, and Ruth loved her dearly. Ruth said, "I will stay with you. I will go wherever you go. Your people will be my people. Your God will be my God."

So Ruth left her friends and family to travel with Naomi to the city of Bethlehem. The two widows were very poor. Ruth gathered grain in a nearby field so they would have food to eat.

A rich man named Boaz owned the land. He noticed Ruth working hard in his field. Boaz saw that Ruth was kind and good to her mother-in-law. Boaz married Ruth, and they had a baby boy. Now Naomi and Ruth were happy because God had given them a new family.

Pleasing God

Ruth was kind and good to her mother-in-law, Naomi. And God blessed her helpful attitudes and actions.

How can you show kindness to your family members?

Make a *little helper poster*. First, write the days of the week on a posterboard. Now, list several things you can help your parents do around the house, such as keeping your room neat, setting the table, taking out the trash, and putting away toys when you're not playing with them. Keep a chart of the helpful things you remember to do. Ask your parents to help you create a special treat to share with your family at the end of the week (some treat suggestions: ice cream sundaes, brownies, or gelatin). You can review the *little helper poster* as you eat the treat.

HELP ME TO FORGIVE OTHERS

When people treat you mean, how do you treat them in return? How does God feel toward us when we misbehave or act badly? How does God want us to act toward the people who mistreat us?

Praise

Repeat the following rhyme:

> *Thank the Lord every day, for taking all my sins away!*
> *Help me, Lord, every day, to forgive in this same way.*

Clap your hands together after saying each syllable in the rhyme. Now repeat the words, clap your hands, and try marching around the room!

Prayer

This prayer is from Psalm 51:1–2, 9–13.

Dear God,
Be merciful to me because You are loving.
Wash away all my guilt and make me clean again.
Turn Your face from my sins and create in me a pure heart.
Give me back the joy that comes when You save me.
Keep me strong.
Then I will teach Your ways to those who do wrong.
In Jesus' Name, amen.

Promise

"Yes, if you forgive others for the things they do wrong, then your
Father in heaven will also forgive you for the things you do wrong."
—MATTHEW 6:14

People in the Bible

Joseph's brothers were mean to him because they were jealous of him. One day Joseph's brothers grabbed him and threw him in a pit. A group of traders passed by.

"Let's sell Joseph to the traders," the brothers said.

The traders took Joseph to Egypt and sold him as a slave.

Many years passed. Joseph worked very hard, and God blessed him. God helped Joseph become an important leader in Egypt.

When a famine came to the land, Joseph's brothers had to travel to Egypt to buy food. They did not know that Joseph was in charge of giving food to the hungry people. Nor did they know they would have to buy food from Joseph.

Joseph recognized his brothers, but he kept quiet until they visited again.

Finally he said, "Brothers, it is I, Joseph!"

The brothers were surprised and frightened.

"Don't be afraid of me," said Joseph. "God turned into good what you meant to be evil."

Joseph forgave his brothers, even though they had been mean to him. Then Joseph helped his brothers so they would have plenty to eat.

Pleasing God

How would you have treated Joseph's brothers? It isn't always easy to forgive people when they treat us badly. But God wants us to forgive others, just as He forgives us.

Try putting on a *forgiving face.* Draw a big smiley face on one side of a paper plate. Make a list of all the people you need to forgive on the other side of the paper plate.

Ask God to help you forgive each one. Remember that God is pleased when we forgive others.

A PRAYER OF FAITH

What is faith? Faith means being sure of the things we hope for. Believing means knowing that something is real, even if we do not see it.

Praise

Say the words from Psalm 111:1–4 aloud to the Lord:

> *I will thank the Lord with all my heart. . . . The Lord does great things. . . . What He does is glorious and splendid. His goodness continues forever. His miracles are unforgettable. . . .*

Now thank God for some of the great things He has done:

I thank You, Lord, for creating this world.

I thank You, Lord, for making me!

I thank You, Lord, for _____.

61

Prayer

This prayer is based on Mark 11:22–24 and Ephesians 1:18–20.

Lord,
You told us to have faith in God. You said if we believe that what we ask for will happen, then God will do it.

Help me to have a greater understanding of Your ways. And help me to realize how great God's power is to those who believe! Amen.

Promise

"'So I tell you to ask for things in prayer. And if you believe that you have received those things, then they will be yours.'"

—MARK 11:24

People in the Bible

A man named Jairus bowed before Jesus. He begged, "Please heal my little girl. She's dying!"

Jesus went with Jairus, and many people followed. In the crowd was a woman with a blood disease. No one could cure her.

The woman had heard about Jesus' miracles. She believed Jesus could heal her if she could just touch Him through the crowd.

The woman came up behind Jesus as He walked with Jairus. She touched the edge of Jesus' coat. Instantly she was healed.

"Who touched Me?" asked Jesus.

The frightened woman stepped forward. "I did," she said.

Jesus said, "You are healed because you believed."

At the same time, a messenger hurried to Jairus.

"Your daughter is dead!" he cried.

Jesus told Jairus, "Do not be afraid; only believe." At Jairus's house, Jesus held the little girl's hand. He said, "My child, stand up!"

Jairus's daughter stood up. She was well!

Pleasing God

Try making a *prayer box*. Write your prayer requests on strips of paper. Drop them into a shoe box. You may want to decorate the box.

Later, read over your prayers. Have faith that God will answer them. Thank God for all the answered prayers.

A PRAYER IF I POUT OR COMPLAIN

God wants us to sing praises to Him and to say kind words to one another.

He wants us to be happy with what we have, rather than complain about what we don't have.

Praise

O, Be Careful

2. O, be careful, little mouth, what you say . . .
3. O, be careful, little ears, what you hear . . .
4. O, be careful, little hands, what you do . . .
5. O, be careful, little feet, where you go . . .

67

Prayer

This prayer is from Psalm 141:3–4.

Lord, help me control my tongue;
Help me be careful about what I say.
Don't let me want to do bad things anywhere I go.
Amen.

Promise

"I will praise you, Lord, with all my heart.
I will tell all the miracles you have done.
I will be happy because of you.
God Most High, I will sing praises to your name."

—*PSALM 9:1–2*

People in the Bible

After the Israelites left Egypt, they started complaining about all their troubles in the desert. God was not pleased because they had forgotten to be thankful for all the miracles He had done for them.

Then fire burned up part of their camp, and the people cried out to Moses for help.

When Moses prayed, the fire stopped. But God's people didn't stop complaining.

They complained about having no meat to eat. So God sent them quail to eat.

The people had to eat quail every day for a month. And they hated it. They were sorry they had ever grumbled about their food.

Pleasing God

Practice being a "praiser" rather than a "pouter" by singing a song of praise to God. Try adding an instrument while you sing. You can make a drum out of an empty coffee can. You could make a tambourine sound by tapping a pie tin.

Sing the "O, Be Careful," chorus again and add some actions. Cover your eyes when you sing the first verse. Cover your mouth when you sing the second verse, and so on. Cover your ears . . . pray with your hands . . . point to your feet. . . .

A PROMISE WHEN I SHARE

Name some of the wonderful things God has blessed you with. What do you have that you can share with someone? It pleases God when we give to others.

Praise

Give, and It Will Be Given

Angela Abraham

Angela Abraham
Arr. Allan Koppelberger

Give, and it will be giv-en un-to you; Pressed down, shak-en up and

o - ver - flow - ing, too. Give, and it will be giv - en back a - gain; The

meas - ure used for oth - ers will be giv - en back times ten!

Prayer

Dear Lord,
You've blessed me with a lot to share.
So please make me aware
Of the young and the old
Who are needy or cold.
And help me to give what I've got
To those who have not.
Let me show that I care
With what I have to spare.
In Jesus' Name, amen.

Promise

"Give, and you will receive. You will be given much. It will be poured into your hands—more than you can hold. You will be given so much that it will spill into your lap. The way you give to others is the way God will give to you."

—LUKE 6:38

People in the Bible

Elijah was a prophet. God sent Elijah to the home of a poor widow. Elijah asked the woman for a cup of water and a piece of bread.

"All I have is enough flour and oil to make one last meal for my son and me," she said.

"Don't worry," Elijah said. "Trust God to take care of you."

"First, bake me a small loaf of bread, then cook for yourself," said Elijah. "The Lord says your jar of flour will never become empty, and the jug will always have oil in it."

The woman did what Elijah told her. The woman shared her little bit of bread, and the Lord blessed her with more. The jar of flour and the jug of oil were never empty.

So Elijah, the widow, and her son had enough food for each day.

Pleasing God

Think of some children who are poor or in need. Maybe you have clothes or toys you can share with them.

Ask your parents if you can create a *care box* of clothes and toys to give these children. Then go with your parents to deliver the donations.

A PRAYER IF I ARGUE OR FIGHT

What do you argue about? How do you feel when you fight? Does it matter to God whether you are right or wrong when you argue?

Praise

Read aloud:

> *Lord, I praise You because You are kind and You show us mercy. You do not become angry quickly. You are full of love. You listen to my prayers for help when I argue with my friends and family. Thank You, Lord, for changing our angry hearts into forgiving hearts of love, just like Yours. Thank You for my friends and family.*

Prayer

"He's wrong! I'm right!"
Push and pull,
Scream and fight.
Lord, I know this isn't pleasing to Your ears.
Please forgive me for yelling,
And dry away these angry tears.
Please help me to get along with others.
Help me to stop fighting with my sisters and my brothers.
In Jesus' Name, amen.

Promise

"Never shout angrily or say things to hurt others. Never do anything evil. Be kind and loving to each other. Forgive each other just as God forgave you in Christ."

—EPHESIANS *4:31–32*

People in the Bible

One day, Jesus overheard His disciples fighting about something.

"What are you arguing about?" Jesus asked His followers.

But the men were ashamed and did not answer. Their argument was about which one of them was the greatest.

Finally, one of Jesus' followers asked Him, "Who is greatest in the kingdom of heaven?"

Jesus called a small child to His side.

Jesus said, "You must change and act like this child, who loves and obeys Me. If you don't do this, you will never enter the kingdom of heaven. The greatest person in the kingdom of heaven is the one who makes himself humble like this child. Do not think children have little value. Children are very important to God. I tell you that they have angels in heaven who are with My Father always!"

Pleasing God

Next time you get into a fight with a friend, try to be the first to make up. Remember to say, "I am sorry. Will you please forgive me?"

You can practice making up right now, by giving someone a great big hug! Then take turns drawing a picture together. Tell a story about the characters each of you adds to the picture.

I PRAISE GOD FOR BLESSINGS

Do you like to hear good things about yourself? So does God! Saying nice things about God is called praise. God loves for us to praise Him.

Praise

Doxology

Thomas Ken (1637–1711)

Louis Bourgeois (1510–c. 1561)
Arr. Allan Koppelberger

Praise God from whom all bless-ings flow, Praise Him, all crea-tures here be - low. Praise Him a - bove, ye heav'n-ly host, Praise Fa-ther, Son, and Ho-ly Ghost. A - men.

Arrangement copyright © 1995 by House of Abraham

82

Prayer

God Bless

God bless all those that I love,
God bless all those that love me,
God bless all those that love those that I love,
And all those that love those that love me.
                    —*New England Sampler*

Promise

"The Lord remembers us and will bless us. . . .
The Lord will bless those who fear him,
from the smallest to the greatest."
                    —*Psalm 115:12–13*

83

People in the Bible

Many people brought their children to Jesus so He could
pray for them. Jesus' followers thought He was too busy
teaching to bother with babies. But Jesus said, "Let the little
children come to me!" Then He held the children and
blessed them.

Pleasing God

List some of the things God has blessed you with. Here are
a few things to help you get started:

     1. Friends

     2. Food

     3. Healthy bodies

     4. Home

     5. _____

Memorize the *God Bless* prayer (page 83) and practice
saying it often.

I THANK GOD FOR SUNSHINE OR RAIN

Not every day is bright and sunny. Some days are dark and dreary. But you can thank and praise God, no matter what the weather is outside or how you feel inside.

Praise

Heavenly Sunshine

Henry J. Selley 1859-1942

George H. Cook ? - 1948;
Arr. Allan Koppelberger

Heav-en-ly sun-shine, heav-en-ly sun-shine Flood-ing my soul with glo-ry di-vine; Heav-en-ly sun-shine, heav-en-ly sun-shine Hal-le-lu-jah, Je-sus is mine.

Arrangement copyright © 1995 by House of Abraham

Prayer

Dear Lord,
In sunshine or rain
You never change,
So I'll praise You the same,
And Your promises claim.
Next time I'm feeling blue,
I know what to do.
I'll lift up Your Name,
And I'll praise You again!
Amen.

Promise

"The heavens tell the glory of God. And the skies announce what his hands have made."

—PSALM 19:1

People in the Bible

God told Noah, "I will flood the earth with water. You will be saved if you obey me."

God told Noah to build a big boat called an ark. Noah did everything God said. Noah built a boat tall and wide. His family and many animals could ride safely inside. Alligators, elephants, monkeys, and bears—pairs of every animal—marched onto the ark. Then God tightly shut the door.

Lightning flashed. Thunder crashed! Rain poured from the sky. It stormed for forty days and nights. The water rose high above the mountain peaks.

Finally, God sent a wind to dry the earth. After many days, the ark touched solid ground. When Noah left the ark, he thanked God for saving his family. God was very pleased. He blessed Noah.

God said, "The earth will never again be destroyed with a flood. A rainbow in the sky will be a sign of My promise to you."

Pleasing God

Remember, Noah trusted God through the flood. He thanked God for saving him and his family.

What do you like to do on a sunny day?

What do you do on a rainy or cloudy day?

Next time it is dark or dreary, have a Noah's ark puppet show! Draw faces on paper lunch bags. Make Noah and some of the animals that were in the ark (lions, bears, giraffes, zebras, cows, lambs, and others). You can decorate your paper puppets with construction paper, felt, yarn, markers, or crayons. When you finish making the puppets, put on a show.

HELP ME TO BE BRAVE

Doesn't it make you feel taller and stronger when your daddy or your mommy picks you up?

God has "strong arms" like that. He promises to lift us up when we ask for His help. He makes us feel brave as we trust Him.

Praise

Sing this chorus to the tune of "Here We Go 'Round the Mulberry Bush."

Our God Is Great and Glorious

Our God is great and glorious.
His ways are all-victorious.
Children come before the King.
And lift our voices, let them sing.
(Repeat)

91

Prayer

This prayer is rewritten from Psalm 18:1–3.

Dear Lord,
I love You. You are my strength. You are my protection. When I need help, I can run to You for safety because You are like a high tower. You give me courage and strength.
Thank You for answering my prayer for help when I call Your Name, amen.

Promise

"'Remember that I commanded you to be strong and brave. So don't be afraid. The Lord your God will be with you everywhere you go.'"

—JOSHUA 1:9

People in the Bible

The Lord told Joshua to cross the Jordan River and lead the children of Israel into the Promised Land.

The Lord said, "Joshua, be strong and brave! Do not be afraid. I will be with you everywhere you go."

Joshua told the people, "Tomorrow, God will do amazing things."

The Israelites prayed. They believed God would perform a miracle for them to enter the Promised Land.

The next day, Joshua told the priests to go to the river and step into the water. The brave priests obeyed Joshua. They carried the Holy Box from the Holy Tent to show that God was with them.

At the moment they stepped into the river, the water stopped flowing! All the people of Israel crossed the Jordan River on dry ground.

Pleasing God

If it's hard for you to be brave in front of other people, try this—sing a solo or recite a poem for your family or a group of people.

Maybe you could try this at church or school.

Ask God to give you courage.

LISTEN TO GOD'S VOICE

How do you think God speaks to you? Would you know His voice if you heard it? God wants to talk to you every day. You are very special to God.

Praise

These Are My Hands

Angela Abraham
Allan Koppelberger

Allan Koppelberger

These are my hands, and with my hands I will praise Him. ___

This is my mouth, and with my mouth I will thank Him. ___

These are my ears, and with my ears I will lis-ten. ___

And with my heart, Lord, I will be faith-ful-ly Yours. ___

Prayer

Dear Lord,
Help me to hear Your voice when You speak to me. Please help me to
answer You quickly. Help me to listen and obey Your Word.
In Jesus' Name, amen.

Promise

". . . Speak Lord. I am your servant, and I am listening."
                    —*1 SAMUEL 3:10*

People in the Bible

One night little Samuel was sleeping in the Holy Tent. A voice called his name. Samuel ran to Eli, the priest and said, "Here I am. What do you want me to do?"

Eli said, "I didn't call you. Go back to bed." Samuel went back to bed. Soon he heard the voice calling him again. Samuel rushed to Eli's side. "I am here. You called me," he said.

"No, Samuel, I didn't call you," Eli said. "Go lie down." Eli
realized the Lord was calling Samuel. Eli said, "When you
hear the voice again, say, 'Speak, Lord. I am listening.'" So
the Lord spoke to Samuel. And Samuel listened to the
Lord's voice.

Pleasing God

The main way God will speak to you is through His Word, the Bible. God will also speak to you as you pray. God may speak to you through dreams. Often, you can hear God's voice when the pastor preaches God's Word. Sometimes God speaks to your heart when you praise Him in song. When you hear God speak, it is important to listen and obey.

A PROMISE OF PROTECTION WHEREVER I GO

Did you know God will protect you everywhere you go?

Ask Him to take care of you and to watch over you. At home or away, at school or at play—God always knows where you are. He has His angels watching over you every day.

Praise

He Leads Me

Joseph H. Gilmore (1834–1918)

William B. Bradbury (1816–1868)
Arr. Allan Koppelberger

He leads me, — He leads — me; by His own hand He leads — me. His

faith-ful fol-low-er I will — be, for by His hand — He — leads me.

Arrangement copyright © 1995 by House of Abraham

101

Prayer

Protect me, O Lord;
My boat is so small,
And Your sea is so big.
            —BRETON FISHERMAN'S PRAYER

Promise

"The Lord protects you as the shade protects you from the sun. . . .
The Lord will guard you as you come and go, both now and forever."
            —PSALM 121:5, 8

People in the Bible

One day, Jacob and his family were traveling home. Jacob got news that Esau, his angry brother, was nearby.

Esau led an army of fighting men. Jacob feared for his family's safety. Jacob prayed, "Lord, You said You would watch over me! I am afraid Esau will kill us! Please protect us."

Jacob prepared a special gift of many animals for Esau.
Jacob thought, *Esau might not fight with me, if he sees this gift*. Jacob prayed again for God's protection.

When Jacob saw Esau, Jacob bowed low before him. Esau
was no longer angry. He ran to Jacob and hugged him.
Esau was happy to see his brother. God had heard Jacob's
prayer. God protected Jacob's family as they traveled.

Pleasing God

Make a *handprint chain*. Trace your hand several times on a sheet of paper. Cut out your handprints. Glue your paper hands side by side on colored construction paper. This picture will remind you that God will hold your hand wherever you go. He promises to protect you with His own hand!

I PRAISE GOD AT CHURCH

Why do you go to church? Who do you learn about at church? What do you do during the church service? Why?

Praise

Joyful, Joyful, We Adore Thee

Henry Van Dyke (1852-1933)

Ludwig Van Beethoven (1770-1827)
Arr. Allan Koppelberger

1. Joy-ful, joy-ful, we a-dore Thee, God of glo-ry, Lord of love;
2. All Thy works with joy sur-round Thee, Earth and heav'n re-flect Thy rays,

Hearts un-fold like flow'rs be-fore Thee, Open-ing to the sun a-bove.
Star and an-gels sing a-round Thee, Cen-ter of un-bro-ken praise;

Melt the clouds of sin and sad-ness; Drive the dark of doubt a-way;
Field and for-est, vale and moun-tain, Bloss'm-ing mea-dow, flash-ing sea,

Giv-er of im-mor-tal glad-ness, Fill us with the light of day!
Chant-ing bird and flow-ing foun-tain, Call us to re-joice in Thee.

Arrangement copyright © 1995 by House of Abraham

106

Prayer

This prayer is based on Psalms 84, 119, 149, and 150.

Lord, the people who go to Your house of prayer are happy. One day in the house of God is better than a thousand days anywhere else! I will praise and worship the Lord in the house of God.

I will sing praises to Your Name. I will praise You for Your power and strength. I will praise You for Your great love. God, I will praise You with all my heart. Your praises will be in my thoughts and on my lips. Lord, help me to follow Your commands and obey Your teaching when I hear Your Word. In Jesus' Name, amen.

Promise

"Happy are the people who live at your Temple. They are always praising you."

—Psalm 84:4

People in the Bible

On the Sabbath day, Jesus went to the house of God. He read God's Word to the people.

He said, "The Spirit of the Lord is in Me. God has chosen Me to tell the Good News. He has sent Me to help the sinners and to heal those who are hurting."

Then Jesus began to explain God's Word to the people. All the people praised Jesus. They were amazed at the beautiful words He spoke.

Later, Jesus went to the temple in Jerusalem. He told the people, "My temple will be called a house of prayer." Then Jesus taught in the temple. He healed blind and crippled people there. And the children sang praises to Him: "Hosanna to the Son of David!"

The religious leaders asked Jesus, "Do You hear what the children are saying?"

Jesus answered, "Yes. Haven't you read the Scriptures? It says, 'You have taught children and babies to sing praises.'"

Pleasing God

Jesus went to church on the Sabbath day. He read God's Word. He prayed and worshiped in the house of God. You can follow Jesus' example by going to church to praise and worship God.

Draw a picture of a church building with open doors. This picture will remind you that the church is God's house.

Try this "Here Is the Church" action rhyme:

Here is the church (*fold your hands with your fingers pointing inside toward your palms*).

Here is the steeple (*place index fingers up; touch them together*).

Open the doors (*wiggle your thumbs back and forth*).

And see all the people (*wiggle your fingers inside*).

110

I PRAISE GOD AT HOME

What does your house look like? How many people live with you there? You may want to draw a picture of your home.

Does Jesus live in your house? Can you worship God at home? How?

Praise

He Is So Precious

Andrea Marceé
Allan Koppelberger

Arr. Allan Koppelberger

He is so pre-cious to me, Je-sus the Al-might-y.

I will ex-alt — Him, I will a-dore — Him; He is so pre-cious to me.

Copyright © 1995 by House of Abraham

111

Prayer

Lord Jesus,
Help us build our house, we pray,
With faith and trust in God today.
Help us fill this house we share
With joy and peace and loving care.
When the winds and rain assail,
Let our little house prevail.
Please give us shelter from the storm,
And keep the fire in our hearth warm. Amen.

Promise

" . . . You must respect the Lord and serve him fully. . . . You must decide whom you will serve. . . . As for me and my family, we will serve the Lord."

—*JOSHUA 24:14–15*

People in the Bible

One day Jesus sat on a hillside and taught His followers.

"Everyone who loves and obeys Me is like the wise man who built his house on rock," Jesus said. "The rain poured, the water rose, and the wind beat against the house. But the house did not fall because it was built on rock."

"The person who does not serve or obey Me is like a foolish man who built his house on sand," Jesus said. "Then the storm came, the water rose, and the wind hit the house. The house fell with a big crash."

Pleasing God

Sing this song:

The Wise Man and the Foolish Man

The wise man built his house upon the rock (repeat 3 times),
And the rains came tumbling down.
The rains came down, and the floods came up (repeat 3 times),
And the house on the rock stood firm.

The foolish man built his house upon the sand (repeat 3 times),
And the rains came tumbling down.
The rains came down, and floods came up (repeat 3 times),
And the house on the sand went SMASH!

Add the following actions: 1. Pound one fist in the palm of the other hand (*building a house*). 2. Raise arms, then lower them, wiggling fingers (*rain*). 3. Raise palms upward (*floods*). 4. Touch fingertips together to form a roof (*house on rock stands*) or clap hands together (*house on sand falls*).

Try building your own house out of sand in a sandbox. Pour a cup of water over the house. Watch how quickly the house falls. Now try building a house with rocks or stones. Pour a cup of water over the stone house. Does the house fall?

I PRAISE GOD IN THE MORNING

What do you do first thing in the morning? Do you remember to pray before beginning your day? God wants His children to start each day with praises and prayers to Him.

Praise

This Is My Father's World

Maltbie D. Babcock (1858–1901)

Franklin L. Shepperd (1852–1930)
Arr. Allan Koppelberger

1. This is my Fa-ther's world, And to my lis-t'ning ears
2. This is my Fa-ther's world– The birds their car-ols raise.

All na-ture sings, and 'round me rings The mu - sic — of the spheres.
The morn-ing light, the li - ly white, De-clare— their— Mak-er's praise.

This is my Fa-ther's world! I rest me in the thought
This is my Fa-ther's world! He shines in all that's fair;

Of rocks and trees, of skies and seas His hand — the — won-ders wrought.
In rus-tling grass I hear Him pass He speaks— to me ev - 'ry - where.

Arrangement copyright © 1995 by House of Abraham

Prayer

Good morning, Lord.
You are greatly adored in heaven and earth.
The sun reflects the glory of Your face
And rises to honor Your grace.
The wind whispers Your name,
And the flowers speak of Your fame.
Just as the birds sing Your praise,
I will worship You all of my days!

Promise

". . . I will wake up the dawn. Lord . . . Your love is so great that it is
higher than the skies. Your truth reaches to the clouds. God, you are
supreme over the skies. Let your glory be over all the earth."

—Psalm 108:2–5

People in the Bible

Long ago God made the world. The earth was dark. The sky
was empty and black. But God's Spirit looked over the
world. He had a wonderful plan! When God spoke, the
heavens appeared. He blessed the earth with beauty. God
shaped the high mountains. He filled the lakes with cool
water.

God made the soft grass, fresh fruit, and bright flowers that smell sweet. He told the sun to shine in the day and the stars to twinkle at night. God made fish to splash and swim in the seas. He made birds to sing and fly through the air. Then He filled the earth with animals:

Some that crawl and creep.
Some that jump and leap.

God said, "Let Us make someone to care for My wonderful world!" God molded a man from dirt and breathed life into him. God named the man Adam. Then God formed a woman to help Adam. Her name was Eve. God placed Adam and Eve in a beautiful garden called Eden. In six days, God made every good thing. On the seventh day, He rested from all His work.

Pleasing God

Sing these words to the tune of, "London Bridge Is Falling Down."

> *In the morning I will rise happily with open eyes;*
> *And wherever I may go, I'll see God's glory.*
> *In the morning I will rise happily with open eyes;*
> *I'll see beauty everywhere; Praise the Creator!*
> —ANGELA ABRAHAM

You can use the following actions while singing this song: *Yawn* and *stretch* your arms over your head, *smile*, and *close and open your eyes wide*. Then finish the chorus by *marching around the room*.

A PRAYER AT DAY CARE OR SCHOOL

What are you learning about in school? Have you asked God to help you during school? God promises to give us wisdom and understanding when we pray for His help.

Praise

This action rhyme is based on Proverbs 3.

Trust in God with all your heart (*cross hands over heart*).

From His Word do not depart (*hold palms upward as though you are holding a Bible*).

Ask God to guide you everyday (*fold hands together in prayer*).

Where you go, and what you say (*drop your hands to sides, march in place, point to mouth*).

Trust in the Lord, today! (*shout and clap three times*).

He will send success your way! (*raise hands heavenward, praise God*).

122

Prayer

A Prayer at School

Sometimes I wish my friends
Could see You with them.
Help my friends know Your ways;
Oh, help them to hear Your words today.
On the playground or during school,
Lord, let me teach them about Your rules!

Promise

"But if any of you needs wisdom, you should ask God for it. God is generous. He enjoys giving to all people, so God will give you wisdom. But when you ask God, you must believe. Do not doubt God. . . ."

—JAMES 1:5–6

People in the Bible

In Babylon, King Nebuchadnezzar asked for four young men from Judah to serve in his palace. Daniel and his three friends were chosen. For three years, they studied hard to learn the king's language. And God helped them. God gave these four men wisdom and the ability to learn. Every time the king asked them something important, they showed great understanding. The king discovered that Daniel and his friends were wiser than all the magicians and fortune-tellers in the kingdom.

Pleasing God

Ask God to give you a better understanding of His Word.

Make your own *God Is with Me Book*. Fold several pieces of construction paper in half. Place them together and attach them with a staple. Or punch a hole through the pages and tie them together with a small piece of yarn. Cut out magazine pictures of places to go and things to do. Glue the pictures in your *God Is with Me Book*. Then write the following Bible verse in your book: "Depend on the Lord. Trust him, and he will take care of you," Psalm 37:5.

A PRAYER FOR RECESS AND PLAYTIME

What do you like to do during playtime? Do you remember to think about God and His Word, when you rest?

Praise

Jesus, from Thy Throne on High

Jesus, from Thy throne on high,
Far above the bright blue sky,
Look on me with loving eye;
Hear me, Holy Jesus.

Be Thou with me every day,
In my work and in my play,
When I learn and when I pray;
Hear me, Holy Jesus.
—THOMAS B. POLLOCK

126

Prayer

Dear God,
Thank You for playtime. Let my life praise You when I am having fun.
Help me not to forget about Your rules when I play. Please help me
remember to share, to be kind and good, to be patient, and to wait
my turn. Help me to show love and to forgive easily. Help me not to
fight. Let me treat others the way I want to be treated. In Jesus'
Name, amen.

Promise

"Happy is the person who doesn't listen to the wicked. He doesn't go
where sinners go. . . . He loves the Lord's teachings. He thinks about
those teachings day and night."

—Psalm 1:1–2

127

People in the Bible

God led the people of Israel out of Egypt to the edge of the Red Sea. The Israelites were terrified when they saw the Egyptian king's army racing after them. But God performed a miracle to save His people from the Egyptian army. He caused the water of the Red Sea to separate, and the Israelites were able to cross the sea on dry land. When the Israelites got to the other side, the water came back together. God had saved them from the enemy.

The people of Israel were tired from their frightening journey. But now they could rest safely. Moses' sister, Miriam, took a tambourine in her hand. All the women followed her, playing tambourines and dancing.

They sang: "I will sing to the Lord because He is worthy of great honor. He has thrown the horse and rider into the sea. The Lord gives me strength and makes me sing. He has saved me. He is my God, and I will praise Him."

Pleasing God

Even when you rest or play, remember to praise God. Try making your own play dough (ask a parent to help you):

4 cups flour
2 cups salt
1/4 cup vegetable oil

3 tablespoons cream of tartar
4 cups cold water
(add food coloring if desired)

Mix together the flour, salt, and cream of tartar. Add enough water to make the mixture resemble soft gravel. Finally, add the oil, then mix until thoroughly blended. A few drops of food coloring can be added. Place the mixture in a sauce pan and cook on a stovetop at a low temperature. Stir the mixture constantly until it thickens. Remove the mixture from the heat and allow it to cool. Knead the thickened mixture as though you are making bread dough.

Now, use your imagination and have lots of fun with your own play dough! You can make a variety of shapes (animals, flowers, stars, people, etc.). Think about the things God shaped with His own hands when He created the world!

I THANK GOD BEFORE MEALS

Do you remember to say "please" and "thank you" during mealtime? Do you thank your parents for providing and preparing your meal? It is very important to thank God for your meal!

Praise

For every cup and plateful
God make us truly grateful!
       —TRADITIONAL

Thank You for the world so sweet,
Thank You for the food we eat,
Thank You for the birds that sing,
Thank You, God, for everything!
       —E. RUTTER LEATHAM (1870–1933)

130

Prayer

Dear God,
Thank You for the loved ones at our table.
Please give us good health, and make us able
To praise You for the blessings You bring
At harvest time and through the spring.
For this food now, we humbly bow
To our Father above, who's full of love!
In Jesus' Name, amen.

Promise

"All living things look to you for food. And you give it to them at the right time."

—PSALM 145:15

People in the Bible

One day Jesus and His friends went up on a hill and sat down. Many people followed Jesus. Jesus taught the people all day long. After a while, Jesus told His apostles to feed the people.

Philip answered, "It would take a lot of money to buy food for this crowd!"

One little boy had five loaves of bread and two little fish.

He gave them to Andrew, one of Jesus' helpers.

Andrew told Jesus, "This boy will share his meal, but it's not enough." Jesus said, "Tell all the people to sit down for dinner."

Jesus took the bread and fish. He looked up to heaven and thanked God. Then Jesus divided the food and gave it to His followers. They shared it with the hungry people. Everyone had plenty of food to eat. In fact, there were twelve baskets of food left over.

Pleasing God

Remember to be polite and show thanks to your parents, by taking your plate, cup, and eating utensils, to the sink. They will be glad you helped.

Make a *Thanksgiving Placemat* out of construction paper. After decorating your placemat, cover it with clear contact paper. Now, you can use your *Thanksgiving Placemat,* over and over, again!

A BEDTIME PRAYER

Do you have a favorite bedtime prayer?
Would you like to learn a new prayer?
It will be fun!

Praise

Sing these words to the tune of "Are You Sleeping?"

I Will Trust Him

I will trust Him, I will trust Him.
I won't fear, I won't fear.
I have the faith to close my eyes,
And rest in peace throughout the night.
'Cause I know my God is near.
'Cause I know my God is here!

—ANGELA ABRAHAM

135

Prayer

Good-Night Prayer

Father, unto Thee I pray,
Thou hast guarded me all day;
Safe I am while in Thy sight,
Safely let me sleep tonight.

Bless my friends, the whole world bless;
Help me to learn helpfulness;
Keep me ever in Thy sight;
So to all I say good-night.
                              —HENRY JOHNSTONE

Promise

"The Lord listens when I pray to him. I go to bed and sleep in peace.
Lord, only you keep me safe."

                              —PSALM 4:3, 8

People in the Bible

Jacob set out on a long journey. He was going to live in the land where his grandfather lived.

He had to stop when the sun set. He spent the night in a lonely place. He slept on the ground. And he used a stone for a pillow.

In a dream, Jacob saw angels climbing up and down a ladder to heaven. God was standing above the ladder.

He said, "I will protect you everywhere you go. I will not leave you."

When Jacob woke up, he said, "Surely the Lord is in this place."

Before Jacob continued his journey, he made a promise. "I will give God one-tenth of all He gives me."

Pleasing God

Try singing "I Will Trust Him" before you go to bed. Sing this song to the tune "Are You Sleeping?" Have fun using the following motions.

I (*point to self*) will trust Him (*point heavenward. Repeat*).

I (*point to self*) won't fear (*shake head, "No." Repeat*).

I (*point to self*) have the faith to close my eyes (*close eyes*),

And rest in peace throughout the night (*lean hands against cheek, as though you are sleeping. Keep your eyes closed*).

'Cause I know my God is near (*raise hands heavenward*).

'Cause I know my God is here (*fold hands over your heart*)!

A PROMISE DURING DOCTOR VISITS

Did you know God goes with you when you go to the doctor's office? It will make you feel better to remember that the same God who made your body can heal your body!

Praise

Lift up your hands and praise the Lord as you read aloud these words from Psalm 139.

> *"Lord . . . I praise you because you made me in an amazing and wonderful way. What You have done is wonderful. . . . You saw my bones being formed as I took shape in my mother's body. . . . You saw my body as it was formed. All the days planned for me were written in your book before I was one day old."*

Now clap your hands together and thank God for making you special.

Prayer

This prayer is based on Psalm 139.

Dear Lord,
You know when I sit down and when I get up. You know my thoughts
before I think them. Even before I say a word, You already know what I
am going to say. You know where I go and everything I do. Your
knowledge is amazing to me! If I whisper a prayer quietly, You hear
me. If I think something, You hear it. If I pray in my thoughts without
any words, You still hear me. Please let my thoughts and words always
please You. And be with me today, Lord Jesus. Amen.

Promise

"Do not worry about anything. But pray and ask God for everything
you need. And when you pray always give thanks. And God's peace
will keep your hearts and minds in Christ Jesus. . . . Think about the
things that are good and worthy of praise. . . . And the God who gives
peace will be with you."

—PHILIPPIANS 4:6–9

141

People in the Bible

Hezekiah became sick with a deadly disease. Isaiah the prophet said, "The Lord says you will not get better."

Hezekiah was afraid. He cried to the Lord, "God, please be with me. Lord, remember how I've always tried to obey You." Then Hezekiah asked God to heal him. Hezekiah prayed that God would bless him with a long life.

God gave Isaiah a message for Hezekiah. Isaiah said, "The Lord says you will be healed. God will add many years to your life."

Isaiah told Hezekiah to put medicine on his body. Then Isaiah prayed for Hezekiah. And the Lord healed Hezekiah.

Pleasing God

Thank God for creating you by making a book about yourself.

Join several pieces of paper together with staples or punch holes in the papers and tie them together with yarn. Write "I Am a Child of God" on the cover of your book. Find a photograph of yourself and glue it to the cover. On the second page, write your name, address, and phone number. On the third page, write your birth date, your eye color, and your hair color. Put your fingerprints on the fourth page. Rub your fingers in paint, then press your fingers to the paper. You may want to add a picture of your family to remind you of the people who love you. Draw a picture of Jesus in your book to remind you of God's love. This book will remind you that God made you special and unique!

I PRAISE GOD ON THE MOUNTAINS OR AT THE BEACH

Can you praise God quietly? How?

Do you pray to God when you are with other people?

Praise

This praise is based on Psalm 95:2–7.

While you read it, think about how great the Lord is. Thank God quietly in your thoughts.

> "Let's come to God with thanksgiving. The Lord is great. He is King over all gods. The deepest places on earth are His. And the highest mountains belong to Him. The sea is His because He made it. He created the land with His own hands. Come, let us bow down and worship Him. Let's kneel before the Lord who made us. He is our God. And we are the people He takes care of."

Prayer

Lord, in the Scriptures You have said, "Be quiet and know that I am God." Please help me to be still before You. I want to listen to Your voice and trust Your Word. Let me quiet myself in Your presence. As I think about You, please speak to my heart.

Promise

"God says, 'Be quiet and know that I am God. I will be supreme over all the nations. I will be supreme in the earth.'"

—Psalm 46:10

People in the Bible

One day a crowd of people followed Jesus to Lake Galilee. They wanted to hear the Word of God.

Jesus saw two boats near the shore. The boats belonged to a group of fishermen—Peter, Andrew, James, and John. Jesus got into Peter's boat and taught the people on the shore.

Later, Jesus told Peter, "Put your nets in the deep water, and you will catch fish."

Peter said, "Master, we tried all night, and we didn't catch any fish."

Peter and the other fishermen obeyed Jesus anyway.

They caught so many fish that the nets began to break. The fishermen were amazed at the miracle. Peter bowed before Jesus.

Jesus said, "From now on you will fish for men." The fishermen left their boats on the shore and followed Jesus everywhere.

Pleasing God

You can finish this thanksgiving psalm (Psalm 136:1, 5–6) from your own heart. Try playing charades with a friend or parent. Let someone guess what you are thankful for while you act out the answers!

"Give thanks to the Lord because he is good.
His love continues forever. . . .
With his wisdom he made the skies.
His love continues forever.
God spread out the earth on the seas.
His love continues forever. . . ."

I will give thanks to the Lord for _____.
His love continues forever.
I will praise God at all times because _____.
His love continues forever.
I will praise God when I am _____.
His love continues forever.
I will praise God when I go _____.
His love continues forever.

I PRAISE GOD FOR GIVING HIS WORD

Do you read God's Word every day? Through His Word, God teaches us how to live right. God speaks to our hearts when we read His Word. We know God better when we learn His Word.

Praise

Sing or say the words to the following traditional Bible school song:

The B-I-B-L-E

The B-I-B-L-E,
Yes, that's the book for me,
I stand upon the Word of God,
The B-I-B-L-E.

Prayer

This prayer is based on Psalm 119:33–35, 105, 171–172.

Your word is like a lamp for my feet and a light for my way. Let me praise You and sing about Your promises. Teach me Your commands. Then I will obey Your Word forever. Help me understand Your teaching, so I can obey Your rules with all my heart. In Jesus' Name, amen.

Promise

"The Lord's teachings are perfect. They give new strength. The Lord's rules can be trusted. They make plain people wise. The Lord's orders are right. They make people happy. . . . Keeping them brings great reward."

—PSALM 19:7–8, 11

151

People in the Bible

When the Israelites reached Mount Sinai, God called Moses to the mountaintop. God said, "I am the Lord your God. I brought you out of slavery in Egypt."

Then God gave ten rules to help His people live right. He wrote these commandments on stone tablets.

- I am the only, one true God. Love and worship Me.
- Do not worship or serve any other god.
- Do not curse or swear using God's name.
- Rest on the Sabbath day; keep it holy.

- Honor your father and mother.

- Do not kill people.

- Husbands and wives be faithful to each other.

- Do not steal.

- Do not lie.

- Do not wish for things that belong to someone else.

God told Moses, "I have written My rules. Now you can teach them to the people."

Pleasing God

Every day, remember to read God's Word. Then allow God time to speak to your heart through His Word.

Shout the following "Bible Cheer":

"Give me a B!" (Echo B.) "Give me an I!" (Echo I.)

"Give me a B!" (Echo B.) "Give me an L!" (Echo L.)

"Give me an E!" (Echo E.)

"What does it spell?" (Bible!)

"Say it again, louder." (BIBLE!)

"Who gave you the Word?" (God did!)

"And who should you praise?" (The Lord!)

"Now, give God a loud clap offering of praise!" (Clap hands together.)

Try making *Ten Commandments Tablets* out of cardboard. Write down the ten rules on the cardboard with a marker. Place your tablets on your dresser. Each morning, you can memorize a new commandment. After ten days, recite all ten commandments for your parents. Ask them to help you decide on a special reward for learning God's Word!

I THANK GOD FOR SENDING HIS SON

Have you asked Jesus to be your Savior?

Pray for Jesus to come into your heart.

Praise God for sending His Son to save you.

Praise

Down in My Heart

I have the joy, joy, joy, joy down in my heart, (where?)
down in my heart, (where?) down in my heart.
I have the joy, joy, joy joy down in my heart, (where?)
down in my heart to stay.
And I'm so happy, so very happy,
I have the love of Jesus in my heart.
And I'm so happy, so very happy,
I have the love of Jesus in my heart.

Add the following actions:
1. Clap four times *(joy).*
2. Cross hands over your heart *(heart).*
3. Cup hands and SHOUT *(where?).*
4. Lift hands heavenward *(happy).*

155

Prayer

Jesus, Friend of Little Children

Jesus, friend of little children,
Be a friend to me
Take my hand and ever keep me
Close to Thee.
Teach me how to grow in goodness,
Daily as I grow:
Thou hast been a child, and surely
Thou dost know.
Never leave me, nor forsake me;
Ever be my friend;
For I need Thee, from life's dawning
To its end.

—Walter J. Mathams (1853–1931)

Promise

". . . My soul praises the Lord; my heart is happy because God is my Savior. . . . God has done what he promised. . . ."

—Luke 1:46–47, 55

156

People in the Bible

One day God sent an angel to Mary. The angel said, "Don't be afraid. God has chosen you to be the mother of Jesus. This Holy Child will be the King that God promised. And He will be called the Son of God."

Next, an angel appeared to Joseph in a dream. "Don't be afraid to take Mary as your wife. The baby inside her is from the Holy Spirit," the angel said. "You will call Him Jesus, which means, The Lord Saves."

So Joseph and Mary were married.

The emperor said all the people must go to their birthplaces to list their names and to pay taxes. Joseph and Mary traveled many miles to Bethlehem, their hometown.

Mary was very tired, but there was no place to rest. Bethlehem was crowded with people. Mary and Joseph had to spend the night in a stable.

During the night, Mary's baby was born. She wrapped Him in warm clothes and made a cozy bed for Him in a feedbox.

Some shepherds were watching their sheep in a nearby field. Suddenly an angel appeared. The shepherds were frightened.

The angel said, "Don't be afraid. I am bringing you good news. Tonight your Savior was born in Bethlehem. He is Christ the Lord."

Then a choir of angels sang, "Glory to God in heaven."

Pleasing God

What can I give Him,
Poor as I am?
If I were a shepherd,
I would bring Him a lamb.
If I were a wise man,
I would do my part.
But what can I give Him?
Give Him my heart.

— CHRISTINA G. ROSSETTI (1830–1894)

160

Remember to thank God for sending His Son. At Christmas time try making dough ornaments that show God's love.

2 cups flour	1 cup water
1 cup salt	1 teaspoon alum

Mix the dry ingredients together. Add water to the dry mix. Knead the dough for eight to ten minutes. Form the dough into desired shapes (stars, angels, hearts, lambs, etc.). Poke a hole in the top of the ornament with a toothpick.

Bake on a cookie sheet in an oven at 200 degrees for two hours. (Or, if time allows, the finished craft can air dry, uncovered for several days.) Almost any kind of paint can be used to decorate the dried dough ornaments (oil, tempra, spray paint). Lace ribbon through the hole at the top of the finished ornament. Now it is ready to hang on a Christmas tree.

I THANK GOD FOR THE HOLY SPIRIT

Who is the Holy Spirit?

He is Jesus' presence on earth.

The Holy Spirit helps us learn about Jesus. He helps us pray. He causes us to want to praise the Lord more. The Holy Spirit always points us to Jesus!

Praise

Can't Stop Talkin' 'bout Jesus

Words by Ken and
Angela Abraham

Music by Tink Abraham
Arr. by Allan Koppelberger

Can't stop talk-in' 'bout Je-sus; Can't stop prais-in' His name.

We've been filled with His Ho-ly Spir-it, and we'll nev-er be the same!

Prayer

Dear Jesus,
Please forgive me when I forget to obey You. Thank You for giving Your
life to save me. Please fill me with Your Holy Spirit so You can help me
know how to live right. Let me be a powerful witness for You. I want
everyone to hear about the Good News. Jesus, I want everyone to know
You came to bring new life and hope to the world. Amen.

Promise

"' . . . The Father has made you a promise. . . . The Holy Spirit will
come to you. Then you will receive power. You will be my witnesses . . .
in every part of the world.'"

—*Acts 1:4, 8*

163

People in the Bible

Each day Jesus' followers met together to pray. The believers were waiting for the promise from God. During this time, the believers gathered to celebrate Pentecost. This was the Jewish Harvest Festival. Suddenly a noise came from heaven. It sounded like a strong wind blowing, and it filled the whole house. It looked as though a tongue of fire rested on the head of each believer.

All the believers were filled with the Holy Spirit, and they began to speak in different languages.

Jewish people from every country were in Jerusalem for
Pentecost. They were surprised. "How can this be?" they
said. "We hear these believers speaking in our own
languages about the great things God has done!"

Peter stood up and boldly told the people the good news
about Jesus. "Be baptized in the name of Jesus," Peter said.
"Let Jesus forgive you and save you from sin! Then you will
receive the Holy Spirit too!" The people who believed what
Peter said were baptized. About three thousand people
were added to the the number of believers that day.

Pleasing God

Make your own *Spirit banner*. Draw a beautiful rainbow
with markers on poster board. Sprinkle and glue glitter to
your rainbow. This will remind you of all God's beautiful
promises. Now draw a white dove near the rainbow.
Decorate the dove with felt or feathers. This will remind you
about God's promise to give His Holy Spirit to those who
follow Jesus.

I THANK GOD FOR ANGELS

God made angels to praise Him in heaven and to watch over His children on earth. Most of the time, we cannot see angels. But we know that God sends angels to help us. They go where God sends them. They do what God tells them to do. They come into our homes, churches, and schools. And one even protected Daniel in a lions' pit!

Praise

All Night, All Day

Spiritual

Arr. Allan Koppelberger

All night, all day, an-gels watch-in' o-ver me, my Lord.

All night, all day, an-gels watch-in' o-ver me.

Arrangement copyright © 1995 by House of Abraham

Prayer

Thank You, Father above, for sending angels to guard me with love. It helps me to know that wherever I go and whatever I do, Your angels will follow and watch me there, too!
Amen.

Promise

"He has put his angels in charge of you.
They will watch over you wherever you go."

—PSALM 91:11

People in the Bible

The Bible tells about a brave man named Daniel.

Daniel dared to pray to God even when King Darius made a law that said no one could pray to any god but him. Anyone who disobeyed this law was to be thrown into a lions' pit. Daniel heard about the law. But it did not stop him from praying to the Lord God.

Some men told King Darius about Daniel's prayers.

Poor Daniel was thrown into the lions' pit. The hungry lions came running to eat Daniel. But they could not even open their mouths. God sent an angel to keep them away from Daniel. The next morning, King Darius hurried to the lions' pit. He called, "Daniel, has the God you worship been able to save you?"

"Yes," Daniel answered. "I am safe. God sent an angel to close the lions' mouths."

Pleasing God

Why do you think Daniel refused to stop praying?

Do you pray each day?

Ask your parents to help you remember to pray.

You may want to draw an angel. What do you think your guardian angel might look like? Hang your picture on the refrigerator to help remind you that God's angels are watching over you.

BLESS MY FAMILY

Did you know that God will bless your family when you ask Him?

Praise

The words of the following song can be sung to the tune, "Twinkle, Twinkle, Little Star."

Bless My Little Family

Bless my little family dear;
Keep us safe year after year.
Help us shower those we love;
With lots of kisses, lots of hugs.
Bless my little family dear;
Keep us safe year after year.

Fill the loving home we share
With understanding, tender care.
Keep us faithful every day
In what we do and what we say.
Fill the loving home we share
With understanding, tender care.

Prayer

Dear Lord,
Bless our home with happiness year after year;
And when sadness comes, quickly dry away our tears.
Protect our home with Your great love,
Watching over the ones I love;
For there's no place I'd rather be,
than with my precious family.
Amen.

Promise

"The father of a good child is very happy.
The person who has a wise son is glad because of him. Make your
father and mother happy. Give your mother a reason to be glad."

—PROVERBS *23:24–25*

People in the Bible

Abram worshiped God. His neighbors prayed to false gods.

God told Abram, "Leave this country. Go to a new land, and I will bless you."

Abram obeyed God. He packed all his things and moved.

Then God appeared to Abram and said, "I will give to your family all the land you see."

Abram thanked God.

One night God spoke to Abram in a vision. "Can you count the stars at night? I will bless you with so many children, you will not be able to count them."

Abram believed God.

Later, God changed Abram's name to Abraham. Again God said, "You will be father of many."

Abraham was ninety-nine years old. God said, "Your wife, Sarah, will have a son."

Abraham said, "Sarah and I are too old to have children."

"Is anything too hard for the Lord?" said God. And the Lord remembered His promise.

Isaac was the son born to Sarah and Abraham. Isaac means "laughter."

Pleasing God

"This Is My Family" Finger Play

"Here is my momma, who cares for us all"
(*hold up one index finger*).

"Here is my daddy, who stands proud and tall"
(*hold up middle finger and index finger*).

"Here is my big (or little) brother (or sister)"
(*hold up ring finger, middle, and index fingers*).

"He helps *me* when I fall"
(*hold up little finger with all the other fingers*).

"This is my puppy dog" (*hold out thumb*).

"He wags his tail, when I call" (*wiggle thumb back and forth*).

PRAISE GOD FOR MY FRIENDS

What are the names of your friends?

Do you enjoy doing nice things for your friends?

What is the best thing you can do to help your friends?

Praise

With a friend, do the following clapping routine. As you say each "thank you," praise God for all the friends He has given you.

THANK *(Clap both hands together with your friend's hands.)*

YOU, *(Clap your own hands together.)*

LORD, *(Clap both your knees with your hands.)*

FOR *(Clap your own hands together again.)*

ALL *(Clap opposite hands with your friend.)*

MY *(Clap your own hands together again.)*

FRIENDS. *(Clap opposite hands with your friend.)*

Thank You, Lord for every one. *(Repeat clapping routine)*

Thank You, Lord for my friend _____.

(Repeat clapping routine as you name a friend.)

Prayer

This is a prayer from Philippians 1:9–11.

A Friend's Prayer

This is my prayer for you:
That your love will grow more and more;
That you will see the difference between good and bad
and chose the good;
That you will do many good things with the help of Christ
to bring glory and praise to God.
In Jesus' Name, amen.

Promise

"I thank God every time I remember you.
And I always pray for all of you with joy."

—*Philippians 1:3–4*

People in the Bible

Jesus went to a wedding with His mother, Mary, and some friends.

There wasn't enough wine for the feast. And the bridegroom was upset.

Mary asked Jesus to help.

Jesus said, "Why come to Me?"

But Mary trusted Jesus to do the right thing. She told the servants, "Do whatever Jesus tells you to do."

Jesus told the servants to fill six big jars with water.

When the bridegroom tasted the water, he was surprised. The water had become wine.

Jesus performed this miracle to help His friends.

Pleasing God

Ask your parents if you could make a *prayer album,* with pictures of friends you'd like to pray for. Fold a large piece of construction paper in half to make a prayer book. Fasten the pictures to the construction paper with a stapler or tape. You may want to decorate the cover of your *prayer album* with a photo or drawing. Remember to pray for the friends in your *prayer album* each day.

HELP MY NEIGHBORS

Who are your neighbors? Are the people who live in other lands or countries your neighbors?

Do you pray for the people who live in other countries? Remember to pray for the missionaries and preachers who teach people in other countries about Jesus.

Praise

This Is My Commandment

Traditional
(John 15:12)

Arr. by Allan Koppelberger

This is My com-mand-ment that you love one an-oth-er, that your joy may be full. This is My com-mand-ment that you love one an-oth-er, that your joy may be full. That your joy may be full, that your joy may be full; This is My com-mand-ment, that you love one an-oth-er, That your joy may be full.

Arrangement copyright © 1995 by House of Abraham

Prayer

Lord, I love You with all my heart and soul. Please help me to love my neighbors. Help me to treat them the same way I would like to be treated. Help me remember that my neighbors are everywhere. . . . the people in the house next door. . . . the people who live in other lands or countries. Help me to please You, Lord, by showing love to others. In Jesus' Name, amen.

Promise

"'Love the Lord your God. Love him with all your heart, all your soul, all your strength, and all your mind.' Also, 'You must love your neighbor as you love yourself. . . . Do this and you will have life forever.'"

—Luke 10:27–28

184

People in the Bible

One day a Jewish lawyer asked Jesus, "What must I do to go to heaven?"

"What does God's law say?" asked Jesus.

"Love the Lord with all your heart and your neighbor as yourself," he answered.

"You are right," said Jesus.

"But who is my neighbor?" asked the lawyer.

Jesus told him a story. "Once a traveler was attacked by robbers. They beat him and left him to die in a ditch. Then a priest passed by. But when he saw the injured man, he walked by on the other side of the road."

"Next a temple worker hurried by. He didn't stop to help either. Finally, a foreigner saw the poor man. He bandaged the man's wounds. Then he lifted the man out of the ditch and took him to a safe place."

Jesus asked the lawyer, "Which man was a good neighbor to the hurting stranger?"

"The man who helped him," said the lawyer.

Jesus said, "Go and do the same thing. Take care of the hurting people around you."

Pleasing God

Love God with All Your Soul and Strength

Love God with all your soul and strength
  With all your heart and mind.
And love your neighbor as yourself:
  Be faithful, just and kind.
Deal with another as you'd have
  Another deal with you.
What you're unwilling to receive,
  Be sure you never do.

—ISAAC WATTS (1674–1748)

Choose someone in your neighborhood and pray for them every night for one week. To let them know you care, tell them you prayed for them.

BLESS MY TEACHERS

How does God teach His children?

Do you think of your grandparents, parents, sisters, brothers, and friends as your teachers? List some of your other teachers: Sunday school teacher, preacher, schoolteacher, piano instructor, soccer coach, and others.

Is there anything you can teach? How?

Praise

Do any of your teachers remind you of God? How?

Read the words of Proverbs 1. Can you think of people who do what this scripture says? It describes those who teach wisdom and give understanding. They "teach you what is honest and fair and right." They "teach the ability to think to those with little knowledge." They give "good sense to the young."

Praise and thank God for all your teachers. List them by name:

Lord, I thank You for_____ who teaches me_____. Please bless_____ for helping me learn about_____.

Prayer

You can say the following prayers from Scripture for your teachers:

Lord, give_____ the right words to teach others the good news about Jesus, without fear. (Ephesians 6:19)
Lord, I pray that_____ will have great wisdom and understanding about You. (Colossians 1:9)
Lord, help_____ live the kind of life that pleases You in every way. (Colossians 1:10)
And Lord, please help me to teach_____about_____.

Promise

"Whoever spends time with wise people will become wise. . . ."
—Proverbs 13:20

People in the Bible

Jesus used many stories to teach His followers about God's kingdom.

"A farmer went out to plant seeds," Jesus said.

"As he scattered the seeds, some fell beside the road. The birds came and ate them all."

He said, "Some seeds fell on rocky ground. When they grew, the hot sun burned those little plants because they had short roots. Other seeds fell among weeds that would later choke the growing plants. But the seeds that fell on good soil grew into strong, healthy plants."

The people asked, "What does this story mean?"

Jesus explained, "The seed is the Word of God. Some people hear His Word; then Satan steals it from them. Other people listen but give up easily when problems come. Others let worries and love of money crowd God from their hearts."

Jesus said, "The people who learn about God's teaching and understand it are like the seeds planted on good soil. They grow into beautiful 'plants.' Then they teach others about the good news of Jesus."

Pleasing God

Make a special gift for a favorite teacher. Try making a *Popsicle-stick photo frame.* Glue four Popsicle sticks together to form a square. Decorate the frame by gluing seeds or dry pasta pieces to it. Paint the seeds or dry noodles a bright color. Now tape a photograph of you and your favorite teacher to the frame. Give the framed photograph to your teacher. Thank your teacher for teaching you. Tell him or her how much you appreciate his or her patience while you are learning.

I PRAISE GOD FOR PETS

Do you have a pet? If you could create your own pet, what would it look like? What would you name it? Praise God for filling the world with so many beautiful and different animals.

Praise

All Things Bright and Beautiful

> All things bright and beautiful,
> All creatures great and small,
> All things wise and wonderful,
> The Lord God made them all.
>
> He gave us eyes to see them,
> And lips that we might tell,
> How great is God Almighty,
> Who has made all things well.
> —CECIL FRANCES ALEXANDER (1818–1895)

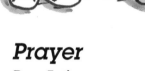

Prayer

Dear Father,
Hear and bless
Thy beasts and singing birds.
And guard with tenderness
Small things that have no words.
　　　　—UNKNOWN

Promise

"God says, 'My people listen to me. . . . I am God, your God. . . . Every
animal of the forest is already mine. The cattle on a thousand hills are
mine. I know every bird on the mountains. Every living thing in the
field is mine. . . . The earth and everything on it are mine."
　　　　—PSALM 50:7,10–12

194

People in the Bible

King Balak was afraid of Israel. He wanted to drive the Israelites back into the desert. He sent a message to the prophet Balaam: "Come and curse Israel. I will give you a great reward."

But God warned Balaam. "Do not curse Israel," He said. "I have already blessed them."

God told Balaam, "Go to Balak. But only do what I tell you." Balaam saddled his donkey and traveled toward Balak's country. God knew Balaam really wanted the reward from Balak.

God sent an angel with a sword to stop Balaam. Balaam's donkey saw the angel but Balaam didn't. The donkey ran off the road. Balaam hit him and forced him back onto the road. The Lord made Balaam's donkey talk.

"Why are you hitting me?" asked the donkey.

Balaam said, "You're making me look like a fool!"

"Have I ever done this before?" said the donkey.

Suddenly Balaam saw the angel and fell to the ground. "I have sinned," said Balaam. "I did not see you blocking the road."

So Balaam blessed Israel instead of cursing them. And God used Balaam's donkey to save Balaam's life.

Pleasing God

It is important to take good care of the animals God placed in the world. If you have a pet, remember to care for it with love. If you don't have a real animal, make a pretend "pet" out of an oatmeal box. What kind of pet would you like? A rabbit? A dog? A cat?

Decorate the box the way you want your pet to look. Color the box with crayons, paint, or markers. Glue buttons or dry macaroni to the box for your pet's eyes. Next, make ears and a mouth for your pet from felt or contruction paper. Add a tail with cotton balls or yarn. Now, name your new pet! Think about how much God must enjoy creating all the different animals in the world.

A PROMISE WHEN MY FRIENDS NEED HELP

Think of some of the ways your friends may be hurting. Maybe someone is in the hospital. Someone else may have a family member or pet that died. Others may feel sad because his or her parents are divorced. What can you do to help your friends when they are hurting? Do you remember to pray for your friends when they need help?

Praise

Evening Hymn

I hear no voice, I feel no touch,
I see no glory bright;
But yet I know that God is near,
In darkness as in light.

He watches ever by my side,
And hears my whispered prayer:
The Father for His little child
Both night and day doth care.
—ANONYMOUS

Prayer

You can pray the following prayers from Scripture for your friends:

Lord, I pray that You will help _____ with Your great power. Please be with _____ so he/she will not give up when sad or bad things happen. (Colossians 1:11)

Lord, You want all people to be saved. You want everyone to know the truth. Please help me to be able to tell _____ about You. I pray that _____ will come to know You as his/her Savior. (1 Timothy 2:4)

Promise

"He heals the brokenhearted. He bandages their wounds."

—PSALM *147:3*

People in the Bible

Jesus often stayed at the home of Mary, Martha, and Lazarus. Jesus enjoyed visiting with His friends. One day the sisters sent a message to Jesus: "Lazarus is very sick!"

Jesus said to His followers, "This sickness is so people can see the power of God and praise Him."

Jesus loved Lazarus, but it was two days before He went to see His friend.

When Jesus got there, Lazarus had died and was buried in a cave.

Martha said, "Lord, if You had been here, my brother wouldn't have died!"

Jesus replied, "He who believes in Me will have life even if he dies." Mary fell at Jesus' feet and cried. Jesus felt very sad. Jesus cried with his friends.

Jesus prayed. Then He said, "Lazarus, come out!" Lazarus walked out of the cave. He was alive again! Many people saw Jesus raise Lazarus from the dead. From then on, they believed in Jesus.

Pleasing God

Jesus felt sad when He heard the bad news about Lazarus. Jesus cried with His friends Mary and Martha and comforted them in their sorrow. Then He gave Lazarus the gift of life.

Be sure to tell your friends that Jesus loves them and wants to help them. And don't forget to show your friends that you love them, too. Let them know that you care about them when they are having problems.

First, you can comfort your friends with kind words of encouragement. Tell them that no problem is too big for Jesus to handle. Next, you can try to help them by giving them something they may need, such as food, clothes, or money. The most important thing you can do when your friends are hurting is to keep on being their friend!

"The Lord will keep his promises. With love he takes care of all he has made."

—PSALM 145:13

INDEX

Bible Heroes

Songs of Praise

"Speak to each other with psalms, hymns, and spiritual songs. Sing and make music in your hearts to the Lord."
—EPHESIANS 5:19

Hymns

Doxology 82
He Leads Me 101
Joyful, Joyful, We Adore Thee ...106
This Is My Father's World..........116

Choruses

All Night, All Day 167
The B–I–B–L–E............................150
Bless My Little Family 172
Can't Stop Talkin' 'bout Jesus 162
Cast Your Cares 36
Down in My Heart......................155
Give, and It Will Be Given 72
God's Love Is Amazing...............1
He Is So Precious.........................111
Heavenly Sunshine......................86
Help Me to Be Kind and Good ...50

If You're Angry/Happy 21
I Will Trust Him 135
In the Morning I Will Rise.................121
O, Be Careful.......................................67
Our God Is Great and Glorious 91
Praise God When I Am Happy...........6
Praise Him! Praise Him!......................40
The Wise Man and the Foolish Man ...115
These Are My Hands...........................96
This Is My Commandment.................183
Whisper a Prayer 26

Scriptures

Acts 1:4, 8 163
Acts 2:1–47..........................164, 165
Acts 9:36–43.......................33, 34
2 Chronicles 32:24 142
Colossians 1:9 189
Colossians 1:10 189
Colossians 1:11 199
Daniel 1 124
Daniel 6 ....169, 170
Deuteronomy 31:1–8........93, 94
Ephesians 1:18–20............62
Ephesians 4:31, 32...........22, 78
Ephesians 5:1, 2.................22
Ephesians 6:19 189

Esther...................................28, 29
Exodus 14–15:21...............128
Exodus 19–24.....................152, 153
Exodus 33, 34.....................152, 153
Genesis 1–2 118–120
Genesis 4 ....23, 24
Genesis 6–9:17 ....88, 89
Genesis 12; 13; 15;
    17; 18; 21:1–7 174–176
Genesis 27:41–46; 28........137, 138
Genesis 32–33:11 ....103, 104
Genesis 37; 39–50 57–59
Hebrews 13:5–6 17
Isaiah 38 142

Subject